The Poetry of Laurence Binyon

Volume VII - London Visions

Robert Laurence Binyon, CH, was born on August 10th, 1869 in Lancaster in Lancashire, England to Quaker parents, Frederick Binyon and Mary Dockray.

He studied at St Paul's School, London before enrolling at Trinity College, Oxford, to read classics.

Binyon's first published work was Persephone in 1890. As a poet, his output was not prodigious and, in the main, the volumes he did publish were slim. But his reputation was of the highest order. When the Poet Laureate, Alfred Austin, died in 1913, Binyon was considered alongside Thomas Hardy and Rudyard Kipling for the post which was given to Robert Bridges.

Binyon played a pivotal role in helping to establish the modernist School of poetry and introduced imagist poets such as Ezra Pound, Richard Aldington and H.D. (Hilda Doolittle) to East Asian visual art and literature. Most of his career was spent at The British Museum where he produced many books particularly centering on the art of the Far East.

Moved and shaken by the onset of the World War I and its military tactics of young men slaughtered to hold or gain a few yards of shell-shocked mud Binyon wrote his seminal poem *For the Fallen*. It became an instant classic, turning moments of great loss into a National and human tribute.

After the war, he returned to the British Museum and wrote numerous books on art; especially on William Blake, Persian and Japanese art.

In 1931, his two volume Collected Poems appeared and in 1933, he retired from the British Museum.

Between 1933 and 1943, Binyon published his acclaimed translation of Dante's *Divine Comedy* in an English version of terza rima.

During the Second World War Binyon wrote another poetic masterpiece *'The Burning of the Leaves'*, about the London Blitz.

Robert Laurence Binyon died in Dunedin Nursing Home, Bath Road, Reading, on March 10th, 1943 after undergoing an operation.

Index of Contents

LONDON VISIONS

POEM I

RED NIGHT

Rolled in a smouldering mist, wrapt in an ardent cloud,
Over ridged roofs, over the buried roar
That comes and goes
Where shadowy London mutters at the core
Of meeting streets interminably ploughed
Through blackness built and steepled and immense

With felt, unfeatured, waste magnificence.
The night shudders and glows.
Ensanguined skies, that lower and lift and change
Each instant! sullen with a spectral rose
Upon the towered horizon; but more near
A lurid vapour, throbbing up the gloom.
Glares like a furnace fume;
Exhausted pallors hover faint and strange;
Dull fiery flushes melt and reappear;
While over all in lofty glimpses far
Spaces of silence and blue dream disclose
The still eye of a star.

Muffled in burning air, so dumb
Above this monstrous ever-trembling hum,
What hide you, heavens? What sombre presences,
What powers pass over? What dim Jegioned host,
What peopled pageantries,
With gleam of arms and robes that crimsoned trail.
In silent triumph or huge mockery hail?
O, is it the tumultuous-memoried ghost
Of some lost city, fabulous and frail.
Stoops over London; Susa, Thebes, or Tyre,
Rebuilded out of mist and fire?
No, rather to its secret self revealed
The soul of London burning in the skies
Her desolations and her majesties!

There, there is all unsealed:
Terror and hope, ecstasy and despair
Their apparition yield.
While still through kindled street and shadowy square
The faces pass, the uncounted faces crowd, —
Rages, lamentings, joys, in masks of flesh concealed.
Down a grimed lane, around a bare-benched room.
Seven shapes of men are sunken, heads upon hands bowed.
— O spent and mad desires, lost in the fiery cloud,
What dungeon fled you from?
Across the river's glittering gloom.
Under the towered chimes, a youth steps, bright

With dream that all the future clothes,
Into this new, enchanted land.
Incessant stream the faces into light!
From his wife's hand
Behold a drunkard snatch the toil-earned pence,
And strike her on the patient face with oaths.
But over trees, upon a balcony.

To a young girl life murmurs up immense
Its strange delight.
And in her pulses to her spirit sings.
Along an alley thronged and flaring
A woman's loud self-loathing laughter rings.
The old prowler leers. Fierce cries a mob incense.
(Still the red Night her stormy heart is baring.)
A bent blind beggar taps along the stones.
The indifferent traffic roars and drones.
Blank under a high torch
Gapes a house-ruin, propped with beams; beneath
Some shadow-guarded and negle6led porch
A girl and boy
(Whence flowered, O Night, yon soft and fearful rose?)
Press timid lips and breathe.
Speechless, their joy.
Hither and thither goes
The homeless outcast; students turn the page
By lamplight; the physician sentences;
Dull-eyed or jovial, tavern-loungers drink;
The applauded actor steps upon the stage;
Mothers with far thoughts watch upon their knees
Where children slumber; revellers stamp and shout;
Long-parted bosoms meet in sobbed embrace;
Hope, behind doors, ebbs from the waiting face;
Locked bodies sway and swell
With pain of unendurable farewell:
No instant, but some debt of terror's paid,
Some shame exacted, measureless love poured out.
Weak hearts are helped, strong men are torn.
Wild sorrow in dear arms is comforted.
The last peace dawns upon the newly dead.
And in hushed rooms is heard wail of the newly born.

What ferments rise and mingle.
Night, on your cloudy mirror! what young fire
Shoots, and what endless lassitudes expire!
Yet out of one flesh wrought,
None separate, none single!
Hater and hated, seeker and sought,
O restless, O innumerable shapes,
Kneaded by one all-urging thought.
That none diverts, that none escapes;
So thirsted for, if not in pride, in shame.
If not with tenderness, with railing curse.
If not with hands that cherish, hands that maim.
Life, how vast! Life, how brief!
Eternally wooed and wooing.

That some would stifle, and some hotly seize,
And some by cunning trap into their mesh,

Or plunder in the darkness like a thief;
And these from rapturous pangs of flesh
Would crush to maddening wine, and these
In still renunciation lure to their soul's ease.
Though never in a single heart contained,
Though depth of it no wisest seer may plumb,
Though height of it no hero wholly gained.
Heavenly and human, twined in all our throes
Of passion that in blind heat overflows
To charge the night with thick and shuddering fume.
And felt in every cry, in every deed
Defaced or freed.
Ah, spent at such a dear and cruel cost, —
Possessed a moment, and then, like yon height
Of stars, clouded in our own selves and lost, —
Lives the supreme
Reality, diviner than all dream.

Now all the heaven like a huge smithy glows.
Hollow and palpitating dusk and glare!
Ah, forge of God, where blows
The blast of an incredible flame, what might
Shapes to what uses there
Each obdurate iron or molten fiery part
Of the one infinite wrought human heart.
In tears, love, anger, beauty and despair
Throbbing for ever, under the red night?

POEM II

THE LITTLE DANCERS

Lonely, save for a few faint stars, the sky
Dreams; and lonely, below, the little street
Into its gloom retires, secluded and shy.
Scarcely the dumb roar enters this soft retreat;
And all is dark, save where come flooding rays
From a tavern window; there, to the brisk measure
Of an organ that down in an alley merrily plays,
Two children, all alone and no one by,
Holding their tattered frocks, through an airy maze
Of motion, lightly threaded with nimble feet.
Dance sedately: face to face they gaze,

Their eyes shining, grave with a perfect pleasure.

POEM III

FEBRUARY TWILIGHT

O Weariness, that writest histories
On all these human faces, and O Sighs
That somewhere silence hears! You have no part,
It seems, in the old earth's deep-flowering heart;
Your way of solace is a different way.

A colour comes upon the end of day.
At this street-corner, budded branches bare
Trace springing lines upon the tender air;
But over the far misty flush one's eye
Lights at an apparition: lo, on high
The little moon! as if she came all fresh
Into this world, where our brief blood and flesh
Is weary of burdens. She has seen all earth's
Most mighty races in their ends and births,
And all the glory and sorrow wrought and sung
Since lips found language; and to-night is young.

POEM IV

THE STATUES

Tarry a moment, happy feet,
That to the sound of laughter glide!
O glad ones of the evening street.
Behold what forms are at your side!

You conquerors of the toilsome day
Pass by with laughter, labour done;
But these within their durance stay;
Their travail sleeps not with the sun.

They, like dim statues without end,
Their patient attitudes maintain;
Your triumphing bright course attend.
But from your eager ways abstain.

Now, if you chafe in secret thought,

A moment turn from light distress.
And see how Fate on these hath wrought.
Who yet so deeply acquiesce.

Behold them, stricken, silent, weak.
The maimed, the mute, the halt, the blind.
Condemned amid defeat to seek
The thing which they shall never find.

They haunt the shadows of your ways
In masks of perishable mould:
Their souls a changing flesh arrays,
But they are changeless from of old.

Their lips repeat an empty call,
But silence wraps their thoughts around.
On them, like snow, the ages fall;
Time muffles all this transient sound.

When Shalmaneser pitched his tent
By Tigris, and his flag unfurled.
And forth his summons proudly sent
Into the new unconquered world;

Or when with spears Cambyses rode
Through Memphis and her bending slaves,
Or first the Tyrian gazed abroad
Upon the bright vast outer waves;

When sages, star-instructed men.
To the young glory of Babylon
Foreknew no ending; even then
Innumerable years had flown,

Since first the chisel in her hand
Necessity, the sculptor, took,
And in her spacious meaning planned
These forms, and that eternal look;

These foreheads, moulded from afar,
These soft, unfathomable eyes.
Gazing from darkness, like a star;
These lips, whose grief is to be wise.

As from the mountain marble rude
The growing statue rises fair.
She from immortal patience hewed
The limbs of ever-young despair.

There is no bliss so new and dear.
It hath not them far-off allured.
All things that we have yet to fear
They have already long endured.

Nor is there any sorrow more
Than hath ere now befallen these,
Whose gaze is as an opening door
On wild interminable seas,

O Youth, run fast upon thy feet.
With full joy haste thee to be filled.
And out of moments brief and sweet
Thou shalt a power for ages build.

Does thy heart falter? Here, then, seek
What strength is in thy kind! With pain
Immortal bowed, these mortals weak
Gentle and unsubdued remain.

POEM V

NARCISSUS

By white St. Martin's, where the fountain shone
And plashed unheard in the busy morning air,
March, with rippling shadow and sudden sun.
Laughing riotous round the gusty square,
From frail narcissus heaped in baskets there
Blew to me, as I passed, its odour keen,
Keen and strange, subtle and sweet;
And lo! all new and green.
Spring for me had entered the stony street.

POEM VI

THE BUILDERS

Staggering slowly, and swaying
Heavily at each slow foot's lift and drag,
With tense eyes careless of the roar and throng
That under jut and jag
Of half-built wall and scaffold stream along.

Six bowed men straining strong
Bear, hardly lifted, a huge lintel stone.
This ignorant thing and prone,
Mere dumbness, blindly weighing,
A brute piece of blank death, a bone
Of the stark mountain, helpless and inert,
Yet draws each sinew till the hot veins swell
And sweat-drops upon hand and forehead start.
Till with short pants the suffering heart
Throbs to the throat, where fiercely hurt
Crushed shoulders cannot heave; till thought and sense
Are nerved and narrowed to one aim intense.
One effort scarce to be supported longer!
What tyrant will in man or God were stronger
To summon, thrall and seize
The exaction of life's uttermost resource
That from the down-weighed breast and aching knees
To arms lifted in pain
And hands that grapple and strain
Upsurges, thrusting desperate to repel
The pressure and the force
Of this, which neither feels, nor hears, nor sees?

POEM VII

THE DESTROYER

He stands on high in the torch glare,
With planted feet, with lifted axe.
Behind, a gulf of crimsoned air;
Beneath, the old wall that gapes and cracks

Tossed fragments crash to dust and smoke.
Exulting life, aloft he stands
And drives his unrepentant stroke,
Nor heeds the havoc of his hands.

Below, one lingers gazing. Why
Within his heart does secret joy
Quivering awaken and reply
To each home-blow. Destroy, destroy?

Lulled in the casual feast of sense.
Awed by the ages' fortress-walls.
Out of its slumber roused, intense,
To the swung axe a demon calls, —

Man's Demon, never satiate.
That finds nought made to its desire;
How shall it to this world be mate, —
To a world of stone, a heart of fire!

POEM VIII

THE GOLDEN GALLERY AT SAINT PAUL'S

The Golden Gallery lifts its aery crown
O'er dome and pinnacle: there I leaned and gazed.
Is this indeed my own familiar town,
This busy dream? Beneath me spreading hazed
In distance large it lay, nor nothing broke
Its mapped immensity. Golden and iron-brown,
The stagnant smoke
Hung coiling above dense roofs and steeples dim.
The river, a serpent pale, my wandering eye
Lightened; but houses pressed to his silver brim.
With charging clouds the sky
Broad shadows threw. And now in a sudden shower
A veil sweeps toward me; violent drops fall hard:
Then softly the sun returns on chimney and tower.
And the river flashes, barred
With shadowy arches; warm the wet roofs shine.
And the city is stricken with light from clouds aglow,
Uplifting in dazzling line
O'er valleys of ashy blue, their wrinkled snow.
I leaned and gazed: but into my gazing eyes
Entered a sharp desire, a strange distress.
East I looked, where the foreign masts arise
In rough sea-breathing reaches of broad access;
And North to the hills, and South to the golden haze.
But nowhere found satisfaction more.
Beneath me, the populous ways
Muttered; but idly vast their troubled roar
Went up; I heard no longer: before me rose
Pale as, at morning, mist from autumn streams.
The longing of men made visible, helpless woes.
Fountains of love wasted, and trampled dreams.
Escaped from hearts of youth, or aged brain.
Hither they floated, hither fled.
Then thou, O city of strife, mother of pain,
Faded'st; and out of the mist a new city
I built in dream, the stones of it raised with tears.

And founded deep in hearts that have richly bled;
But watched, through mightier years.
By towers of faith, and girdled with walls of pity.

THE DRAY

Huge through the darkened street
The Dray comes, rolling an uneven thunder
Of wheels and trampling feet;
The shaken windows stare in sleepy wonder.

Now through an open space,
Where loitering groups about the tavern's fume
Show many a sullen face
And brawling figure in the lighted gloom,

It moves, a shadowy force
Through misery triumphant: flushed, on high
Guiding his easy course,
A giant sits, with indolent soft eye.

He turns not, that dim crowd
Of listless forms beneath him to behold;
Shawled women with head bowed
Flitting in hasty stealth, and children old:

Calm as some conqueror
Rode through old Rome, nor heeded at his heel,
'Mid the proud spoils of war.
What woeful captives thronged his chariot wheel.

THE RAG-PICKER

In the April sun
Shuffling, shapeless, bent,
Cobweb-eyed, with stick
Searching, one by one.
Gutter-heaps, intent
Wretched rags to pick.

O, is this a man? —
Man, whose spirit erect
Trampling circumstance.
Death and evil, can
Measure worlds, nor checked
By fell time and chance.

With undaunted eye.
With a mouth of song.
Front the starry blue? —
(O you passers-by,
Moving swift and strong.
Answer, what seek you?)

Husk of manhood, mere
Shrivel of his kind! —
In a bloodless mask
How the old eyes peer,
With no light behind! —
Mate of his mean task;

Yet this wreckage fill
With a thought, possess
With a faith's empire,
It shall be a will
Mightier than the seas,
Man, more dread than fire!

POEM XI

A WOMAN

O thou that facing the mirror darkly bright
In the shadowed corner, loiterest shyly fond,
To ask of thine own sad eyes a comfort slight.
Before thou brave the pathless world beyond 5

Not first to-night invades thy spirit this wild
Despair, when loneliness stabs thee! Turned, thy face
Trembles, and soft hesitation makes thee a child.
The child thou wast in some far, forgotten place.

Amid things for ever rejected. Thoughtest thou so
From the blankness of life to escape to a region enjoyed.
Glowing, and strange? Yet blank to-night, I know,
Spreads life, my sister; within thee a deeper void.

In all this city, methinks, so charged with pain.
None suffers as thou; desiring what thou dost
With insupportable longing, and still in vain
Desiring, still accepting what thou must.

Where tarries he, Love, the adored one? In fields unknown
Roams he apart, or in sound of a pleasant stream
Sleeps? Nay, dwells he in cloudy rumour alone,
A name, a vision, a sweet, eluding dream?

He lives, he lives, my sister; yet rarely to men
He appears; they touch but his robe, and believe it is he.
But soft, with inaudible feet, he is flown, nor again
Comes soon; rejoicing still to be wayward and free.

A moment, ev'n now, he was near thee: invisible wings
Brushed by thee; and infinite longing, to follow, to find
That vision truth, overcomes thee, — thy heart's sad things
To tell in a trusted ear, on a bosom kind.

Alas! not so he is won: when the last despair
Encamps in thy heart, at last when all seems vain.
Then, perchance, he will steal to thee unaware.
And loose thy tears, and understand thy pain.

POEM XII

THE STORM

Stooping over London, skies convulsed
With thunder moved: a rumour of storm remote
Hushed them, and birds flew troubled. The gradual clouds
Up from the West climbing, above the East
Glowed sullen as copper embossed; against their gloom.
Like ghosts astonished, thronged the steeples white.
Still with absorbed hurry the streets' uproar
Ran, shadowed by strange unquiet, as vaguely pursued.
Lone workers from drear windows looked and sighed.
Nearer drooped the sky's contracted face;
The face of a Titan in punishment heavily bowed.
As painful sweat, the drops fell loud: at last.
With silent shivering flashes of angry flame.
Long stifled, his deep thunder burst and groaned.
Then crawling over, the banks of darkness broke
And loosened splendour showered its arrows abroad.

Now, opposite the retreating storm aghast,
In full-recovered sun, new dazzling clouds,
Alp beyond Alp, glitter in awful snow.
Men stop in the street to wonder. The brilliance runs,
Washing with silent waves the town opprest;
Startles squalid rooms with a sudden smile;
Enters gloomy courts, and glories there.
Strange as a vision the wide expanded heavens
Open; the living wind with nearness breathes
On weary faces of women of many cares;
They stand at their doors and watch with a soothed spirit
The marvellous West asleep in endless light.

POEM XIII

THE PARALYTIC

He stands where the young faces pass and throng;
His blank eyes tremble in the noonday sun:
He sees all life, the lovely and the strong.
Before him run.

Eager and swift, or grouped and loitering, they
Follow their dreams, on busy errands sped,
Planning delight and triumph; but all day
He shakes his head.

POEM XIV

THE SLEEPERS

As a swallow that sits on the roof,
I gaze on the world aloof;

In the silence, when men He sleeping,
I hear the noise of weeping:

The tears, by Day derided,
To tender Night confided.

Ah, now I listen, I cannot delay
In thoughts apart; I must not stay.

The doors are closed and fast: unseen.

With stealthy feet I glide between.

I see the sleepers asleep in their beds,
Negligent arms, motionless heads;

Beautiful in the bloom of slumber.
Peaceful armies without number.

Not here I linger: the sigh of those
That sleep not, draws me with answered throes.

A mother mapping her day of cares,
On her sleeping baby softly stares,

A youth by shameful sorrow torn,
Thinks on the unendurable morn.

By her husband, a wife unhappy lies,
With bitter heart and open eyes.

An old man hears the voice of the wave,
His dear son's cold unquiet grave.

Alone in the lonely, listening night
A child lies still in dumb affright:

The burden of all dark things unknown
Weighs on his trembling heart like stone.

A man remembers his dead love's smile,
And his tranquil courage is quelled awhile.

My heart is heavy with love and pain;
The tears within me oppress my brain.

What shall I tell you, you that ache
And number the laggard hours awake?

O stabbed and stricken, what soothing art
Shall I use to assuage the wounds that smart?

The consolation that, ere I knew
Love and sorrow, I fancied true,

Is faint and helpless, now I find.
As beauty told in the ears of the blind:

And I cannot tell, if I would, the thought

That strengthens me most, when my heart is wrought,

O brother that cannot the days undo.
Could I but the reckoning pay for you!

O mother, sink your head in peace.
And I will your knot of care release.

Dear child, give me your dread to bear:
I hold your hand, I stroke your hair.

It is I, who love you, that watch and keep
Darkness from you, the while you sleep.

I have no counsel; I know not why
In your breasts the arrows burning lie;

I cannot heal your hurts, nor take
The sharp iron out of souls that ache.

O yet, as I watch, the lashes close
A little, the eyes their lids dispose;

The hand that fondly lies in mine
Relaxes; the wearied heads decline.

And now on wings the sorrows flee
From the happy sleepers, hither to me.

O noiseless sorrows, darkly thronging,
My heart is prepared: my tender longing

You alone can appease, with tears.
With pangs, with passion, with shame, with fears.

Feed on my heart that is open and bare.
Feed your fill, sorrow and care:

Take me, pains of all souls forlorn.
For O too swiftly arrives the morn.

POEM XV

MAY NIGHT

Come, let us forth, and wander the rich, the murmuring night!

The shy, blue dusk of summer trembles above the street;
On either side uprising glimmer houses pale:
But me the turbulent babble and voice of crowds delight;
For me the wheels make music, the mingled cries are sweet;
Motion and laughter call: we hear, we will not fail.

For see, in secret vista, with soft, retiring stars,
With clustered suns, that stare upon the throngs below.
With pendent dazzling moons, that cast a noon-day white.
The full streets beckon: come, for toil has burst his bars.
And idle eyes rejoice, and feet unhasting go.
O let us out and wander the gay and golden night.

DEPTFORD

Well is it, shrouded Sun, thou spar'st no ray
To illumine this sad street! A light more bare
Would but discover more this bald array
Of roofs dejected, window patched that stare
From sordid walls: for the shy breath of Spring,
Her cheek of flowers, or fragrance of her hair.
Thou could'st not, save to cheated memory, bring.

Alas! I welcome this dull mist, that drapes
The path of the heavy sky above the street,
Casting a phantom dimness on these shapes
That pass, by toil disfeatured, with slow feet
And sad mistrustful eyes; while in the mire
Children a mockery of play repeat,

Drearly to satisfy their starved desire.
Yet O, what clouds of heaviness deter
My spirit; what sad vacancy impedes!
I am like some far-ventured traveller.
Whom, in a forest vast, entangled weeds
Have hindered; over whom green darkness fills
The inextricable boughs and stifling feeds
A poisonous fear, that sinks on him and chills.

Nor finds he faith, amid the monstrous trees
Rooted in silence, peopled with strange cries
And stealthy shadows (where alone he sees
Rank growths of the hot marsh, but watching eyes
Imagines), to believe the self-same bark

He leans on, lifts to the unclouded skies
Its crest victorious from that cradle dark.

I with like pain and languor am opprest:
Me too a forest upon poison fed.
Me too the marsh and the rank weeds infest.
Almost I trace in the dumb pall o'erhead
A net of stubborn boughs that dimly mesh
The air; I stifle: like a chain of lead
They weigh upon my soul, they bind my flesh.

I cannot breathe: the last and worst despair
Begins to invade me, numbing even desire
That panted for sweet draughts of light and air.
Dumb walls against me with blind heaven conspire:
Incredible the sun seems now, a ghost
I dreamed of in my dreams; unreal fire.
The light is blotted out, the blue is lost.

Was it mirage, the glow I fancied warm
On human cheeks, the beauty of my kind?
I feel it fading from me, a brief charm
Flying at touch. Blow hither, storms of wind!

Strike hither, strong sun, to my dulled heart's core!
Awake, disturb me, lest mine eyes grow blind.
By fatal use to a foul dream resigned.
Accept for Nature's body this, her sore.

POEM XVII

THE BATHERS

Hither, from thirsty day
And stifling labour and the street's hot glare,
To twilight shut away
Beyond the soft roar, under hovering trees,
Hither the gleeful multitudes repair.
And by the open, echoing, evening shore,
On the dim grass, to the feint freshened breeze,
With laughter their delighted bodies bare.

Peaceful above the sunset's burning smoke,
One star and white moon lure the eastern night.
Already tasting of that wished delight
The great elms stir their boughs,

As from the day's hot languor they awoke.
But the gliding cool of water whispering calls
The bathers, in soft-plunging falls,
To overtake its ripple with swift stroke.
Or, pillowing their upward feces, drowse
On undulation of an easy peace;
Miraculous release
Of heavy spirits, laving all desire
With satisfaction and with joy entire.

Strange now the factory's humming wheel, the cry
Of tireless engines, the swift-hoisted bales
Unnumbered; strange the smell of ordered wares
In the shop's dimness: noonday traffic fails
Out of the wave-washed ear; stiff office stool,
And busy hush: and like a turbid dream.
The tavern's glittering fume insensibly
Ebbs with the hot race and the glutted stream
Of labour, thieving the dear sands of youth.
But ever closer, like sweet-tasting truth.
The vivid drench, the yielding pressure cool;
And like a known touch comes the fitful breeze
From murmuring silence: the suspended trees
Above, the wet drops that from hair and beard
Run down the rippled back, are real and sweet.
Warm are the breathing limbs, and the firm feet
Tread lightly the firm ground, or lightly race
To mirthful cries: while Evening, nearer heard
And felt, a presence of invisible things
Inbreathes, as to the nostril keen she brings
The darkling scented freshness of the grass.

O now from raiment of illusion shed
The perfect body moves, rejecting care,
And to mysterious liberty remits
The rejoicing mind, in native pasture fed;
And mates its glory with the priceless air.
The universal beam, whatever fits
Untamable spirits, nor is bought nor sold;
Equalled with heroes old,
That beautifully people the green morn
Of time, and from pale marble, young and wise
Gaze past our hurrying world, our triumphs worn.
And our hearts trouble with their peaceful eyes.

POEM XVIII

THE ESCAPE

Destiny drives a crooked plough
And sows a careless seed;
Now through a heart she cuts, and now
She helps a helpless need.

To-night from London's roaring sea
She brings a girl and boy;
For two hearts used to misery,
Opens a door of joy.

Wandering from hateful homes they came,
Till by this fate they meet.
Then out of ashes springs a flame;
Suddenly life is sweet.

Together, where the city ends,
And looks on Thames's stream.
That under Surrey willows bends
And floats into a dream.

Softly in one another's ear
They murmur childish speech;
Love that is deeper and more dear
For words it cannot reach.

Above them the June night is still:
Only with sighs half-heard
Dark leaves above them flutter and thrill,
As with their longing stirred;

And by the old brick wall below
Rustling, the river glides;
Like their full hearts, that deeply glow.
Is the swell of his full tides.

To the farther shore the girl's pale brow
Turns with desiring eyes:
"Annie, what is it you're wishing now?"
She lifts her head and sighs.

"Willie, how peaceful 'tis and soft
Across the water! See,
The trees are sleeping, and stars aloft
Beckon to you and me.

I think it must be good to walk
In the fields, and have no care;
With trees and not with men to talk.
O, Willie, take me there!"

Now hand in hand up to the Night
They gaze; and she looks down
With large mild eyes of grave delight.
The mother they have not known.

Older than sorrow she appears,
Yet than themselves more young;
She understood their childish tears,
Knew how their love was sprung.

The simple perfume of the grass
Comes to them like a call.
Obeying in a dream they pass
Along the old brick wall;

By flickering lamp and shadowy door,
Across the muddy creek,
Warm with their joy to the heart's core,
With joy afraid to speak.

At last the open road they gain,
And by the Bridge, that looms
With giant arch and sloping chain
Over the river's glooms,

They pause: above, the northern skies
Are pale with a furnace light.
London with upcast, sleepless eyes
Possesses the brief night.

The wind flaps in the lamp; and hark!
A noise of wheels, that come
At drowsy pace; along the dark
A waggon lumbers home.

Slow-footed, with a weary ease,
The patient horses step;
The rein relaxed upon his knees,
The waggoner nods asleep.

"Annie, it goes the country way,
'Tis meant for me and you:
It goes to fields, and trees, and hay.

Come, it shall take us too!"

He lifts her in his arms, as past
The great wheels groaning ride.
And on the straw he sets her fast.
And lightly climbs beside.

The waggoner nods his drowsy head.
He hears no sound: awhile
Softly they listen in sweet dread.
Then to each other smile.

Odours of dimly flowering June,
The starry stillness deep.
Possess their wondering spirits; soon,
Like children tired, they sleep.

The waggon creaks, the horses plod
By hedges clearer seen,
Down the familiar dusty road,
And past a village green.

The morning star shines in the pond:
A cock crows loud, and bright
The dawn springs in the sky beyond;
The birds applaud the light.

But on into the summer morn
Beneath the gazing East,
The sleepers move, serenely borne:
The world for them has ceased.

POEM XIX

MIDSUMMER NOON

At her window gazes over the elms
A girl; she looks on the branching green;
But her eyes possess unfathomed realms,
Her young hand holds her dreaming chin.

Drifted, the dazzling clouds ascend
In indolent order, vast and slow,
The great blue; softly their shadows send
A clearness up from the wall below.

An old man houseless, leaning alone
By the tree-girt fountain, only heeds
The fall of the spray in the shine of the sun,
And nothing possessing, nothing needs.

The square is heavy with silent bloom;
The tardy wheels uncertain creep.
Above in a narrow sunlit room.
The widower watches his child asleep.

POEM XX

ELEONORA DUSE AS MAGDA

The theatre is still, and Duse speaks.
What charm possesses all,
And what a bloom let fall
On parted lips, and eyes, and flushing cheeks!
The flattering whisper and the trivial word
No longer heard,
The hearts of women listen, deeply stirred.
For now to each those quivering accents seem
A secret telling for her ear alone:
The child sits wondering in a world foreknown.
And the old nod their heads with springing tear,
Confirming true that acted dream.
And the soul of each to itself revealed
Feels to the voice a voice reply.
With a leaping wonder, a joy, a fear,
It is I, it is I!
But O what radiant mirror is this that dazzles me.
That my dead rapture holds.
That all my joy unfolds.
That sets my longing free,
My sighs renumbers, my old hope renews?
I have lived in a sleep, I have tasted alien bread,
I have spoken the speech, and worn the robes of the dead;
I have buried my heart away, and none believed.
But now, speak on, and my bonds untie:
At last, it is I, it is I!

POEM XXI

THE CONVICT

By the warm road-side, where chestnut and thorn
The brightness shaded, supine, at ease,
A felon, freed that morn,
Lay idle, and wondered, gazing up through the trees.

O strange no more to be one of a band
Numbered and known; to lose the measure
Of day divided and planned:
To think for the morrow, to choose work or pleasure.

His ear the jostling roar of the street
Amazed: he felt the crowd like a load;
And welcomed, refuge sweet,
Deserted suburb and silent shady road.

For now, with his hands habitual stones
Of the pavement he touched: close to the wall
He nestled, and felt to his bones
The warmth, and the shadow cool on his forehead fall.

And catching a leaf from the chestnut strayed,
He held it, glowing green in the light,
Transparent, with veins inlaid;
And thrust the world and its vastness away from sight.

Children from school, as they passed him, eyed
His shorn temples, and whispering turned
To mock him: he on his side.
Abstracted, his limbs disposed to a slumber earned.

A grave citizen, homeward bound.
Perceived him, as negligent still he lay,
And swerved askance, and frowned.
And crossed to the opposite pavement, and went his way.

But warming him shone the indifferent noon;
And chestnut and thorn on his sleeping head
In the careless glory of June
Scattered their delicate blossom of white and red.

POEM XXII

MARTHA

A woman sat, with roses red
Upon her lap before her spread,
On that high bridge whose parapet
Wide over turbulent Thames is set,
Between the dome's far glittering crest
And those famed towers that throng the west,
Neglectful of the summer air
That on her pale brow stirred the hair,
She sat with fond and troubled look,
And in her hand the roses shook.
Shy to her lips a bloom she laid.
Then shrank as suddenly afraid:
For from the breathing crimson leaf
The sweetness came to her like grief.
Dropping her hands, her eyes she raised,
And on the hurrying passers gazed.
Two children, loitering along
Amid that swift and busy throng.
Their arms about each other*s shoulder.
The younger clinging to the older.
Stopped, with their feces backward turned
To her: her heart within her yearned.
They were so young! She looked away:
O, the whole earth was young to-day!
The whole wide earth was laughing fair;
The flashing river, the soft air,
The horses proud, the voices clear
Of young men, frequent cry and cheer,
All these were beautiful and free,
Each with its joy: Alas, but she!
She started up, and bowed her head.
And, gathering her roses, fled.

Through dim, uncounted, silent days.
She had trod deep-secluded ways;
'Mid the fierce throng of jostling lives.
Whom unrelenting hunger drives
Close to the wall, had stolen by,
Yet could not shun calamity.
Her painful thrift, her patient face.
Could not the world-old debt erase;
Nor gentle lips, nor feet that glide,
Persuade the sudden blow aside.
This morn, when she arose, her store,
Trusted to others, was no more.
No more avail her years of care.
She must her bosom frail prepare,
Exposed in her defenceless age.

Against the world and fortune's rage.
For bread, for bread, what must be done?
She stole forth in the morning sun.
I will sell flowers, she thought: this way
Seemed gentler to her first dismay.
Soon to the great flower-market, fair

With watered leaves and scented air,
She came: her seeking, timorous gaze
Wandered about her in amaze.
The arches hummed with cheerful sound;
Buyers and sellers thronged around;
Lilies in virgin slumber stirred
Hardly, the gold dust brightly blurred
Upon their rich illumined snow,
As the soft breezes come and go.
From her smooth sheath, with ardent wings,
Purple and gold, the iris springs;
Deep-umbered wall-flowers, dusk between
The radiance and the odour keen
Of jonquils, this sad woman's eyes
And her o'erclouded soul surprise.
But most the wine-red roses, deep
In sunshine lying, warm asleep,
Breathing perfume, drinking light
Into their inmost bosoms bright,
Seeming fathomlessly to unfold
A treasure of more price than gold.
Martha, o'ercome by wonder new.
Into her heart the crimson drew;
The colour burning on her cheek,
She stood, in strange emotion weak.
But she must buy. Her choice was made:
Red rose upon red rose she laid.
Lingering, then hastened out, with eyes
Bright, and her hands about the prize.
And quickened thought that nowhere aims.
Soon, pausing above glittering Thames,
She spreads the flowers upon her knees.
Vast, many-windowed palaces
Before her raised their scornful height
And haughtily struck back the light.
She scarcely marked them, only bent
Her fond gaze on the flowers, intent
To bind them in gay bunches, drest
So to allure the spoiler best.
But now, as her caressing hand
Each odorous fresh nosegay planned,

A new grief smote her to the heart:
Must she from her sweet treasure part?
They seemed of her own blood. O no,
I cannot shame my roses so:
I will get bread some other way.
So she shut out all thought. The day
Was radiant; and her soul, surprised
To beauty, and the unsurmised
Sweetness of life, itself reproved
That had so little felt and loved!
O now to love, if even a flower,
To taste the sweet sun for an hour.
Was better than the struggle vain.
The dull, unprofitable pain.
To find her useless body bread.
Stricken with grievous joy, she fled.

She fled, but soon her pace grew faint.
She paused awhile, and easier went.
Often, in spirits wrought, despair,
Not less than joy the end of care,
A lightness feigns: for all is done,
And certainty at last begun.
Martha, with impulse fresh recoiled
From empty years, forlorn and soiled,
Trembled to feel the radiant breeze
Blowing from unknown living seas,
And, rising eager from long fast,
Drank in the wine of life at last.
Now, as some lovely face went by,
She noted it with yearning eye;
She joyed in the exultant course
Of horses, and their rushing force.

At last, long wandering, she drew near
Her home; then fell on her a fear,
A shadow from the coming Hours.
By chance a hawker, crying flowers.
His barrow pushed along the street,
And the dull air with scent was sweet.
As on her threshold Martha stood,
A sudden thought surprised her blood.
Quickly she entered, and the stair
Ascended: first with gentle care
Cooled her tired roses: then a box
Of little hoardings she unlocks.
And brings her silver to the door
And buys till she can buy no more.

Laden she enters: the drear room
Glows strangely; the transfigured gloom
Flows over, prodigal in bloom.
Her lonely supper now she spread;
But with her eyes she banqueted.
Over the roofs in solemn flame
The strong beam of the sunset came.
And from the floor striking a glow
Burned back upon the wall; and lo!
How deep, in double splendour dyed,
Blushed the red roses glorified!
When darkness dimmed them, Martha sighed.
Yet still about the room she went
Touching them, and the subtle scent
Wandered into her soul, and brought
All memories, yet stifled thought.
As in her bed she lay, the flowers
Haunted her through the midnight hours:
'Twixt her shut lids the colours crept;
But wearied out, at last she slept.

Next morning she awoke in dread.
O mad, O sinful me! she said,
What have I done? how shall this end
For me? Alas, I have no friend.
She strove to rise; but in her brain
A drowsy magic worked like pain.
She sank back in a weak amaze
Upon the pillow: then her gaze
Fell on the roses; she looked round.
And in the spell again was bound.
The deep-hued blossoms standing by
With serious beauty awed her eye;
Upward, inscrutable, they flamed:
Of that mean fear she was ashamed.
All day their fragrance in the sun
Possessed her spirit: one by one,
She pondered o'er them, dozing still
And waking half against her will.
Her body hungered, but her soul
Was feasting. Gradually stole
The evening shadow on her bed;
She could no longer lift her head,
Deep on her brain the flowers had wrought;
Now in the dim twilight her thought
Put trembling on a strange attire,
And blossomed in fantastic fire.
She stretched her hand out in the gloom:

It touched upon a living bloom.
Thither she turned; the deep perfume
O'ercame her; nearer and more near.
And now her joy is in her fear.
The lily hangs, the rose inclines.
With incense that her soul entwines.
Her inmost soul that dares not stir.
The gentle flowers have need of her.
Unpitying is their rich desire —
Her breath, her being they require.
O, she must yield! She sinks far down.
Conquered, listless, happy, down
Under wells of darkness, deep
Into labyrinths of sleep,
Perishing in sweetness dumb,
By the close enfolding bloom
To a sighing phantom kissed,
Like a water into mist
Melting, and extinguished quite
In unfathomed odorous night.

At last, the brief stars paling, dawn
Breathed from distant stream and lawn.
The earliest bird with chirrup low
Called his mates; softly and slow
The flowers their languid petals part.
And open to the fragrant heart.
And now the first fresh beam returned;
Bright through the lily's edge it burned
And filled the purple rose with fire.
And brightened all their green attire.
And woke a shadow on the wall.

But Martha slept, nor stirred at all.

POEM XXIII

AUGUST

In drooping leaves of the plane
Hangs blue the early heat;
Stirless, a delicate shade
Sleeps on the parching street.

I wander this listless morning
By the banks of the dazzling river;

On the hot stones lean, where toward me
Lights from the water quiver.

And clasping hands upon eyes,
I plunge my thought in a dream
Of days when the sharp air stung
And the ice crushed cold in the stream;

Vainly! on body and mind
Has the tyrant sim his will:
And to me, on the hot stone leaning.
The city is faint and still,

Is faint as listening sands.
Where, awed by the heavy calm
Of the desert heaven, listens,
For ever alone, the palm.

POEM XXIV

THE FIRE

With beckoning fingers bright
In heaven uplifted, from the darkness wakes,
Upon a sudden, radiant Fire,
And out of slumber shakes
Her wild hair to the night;
Bewitching all to run with hurried feet.
And stand, and gaze upon her beauty dire.

For her the shrinking gloom
Yields, and a place prepares;
An ample scene and a majestic room:
Slowly the river bares
His bank; above, in endless tier,
Glittering out of the night the windows come
To that bright summons; and at last appear,
Hovering, enkindled, and unearthly clear.
Steeple, and tower, and the suspended dome.

But whence are these that haste
So rapt? What throngs along the street that press,
Raised by enchantment from the midnight waste
That even now was sleeping echoless?
Men without number, lured from near and far
As by a world-portending star!

Lo, on the bright bank without interval
Faces in murmuring line,
With earnest eyes that shine,
Across the stream gaze ever; on the wall
Faces; and dense along the bridge's side
Uncounted faces; softly the wheels glide
Approaching, lest they break the burning hush
Of all that multitude aflush
With secret strange desire.
Warm in the great light, as themselves afire,
Thousands are gazing, and all silently!
How to the throbbing glare their hearts reply,
As tossing upward a dim-sparkled plume,
The beautiful swift Fury scares the sky.
The stars look changed on high.
And red the steeples waver from the gloom.
Distantly clear over the water swells
The roar: the iron stanchions dribble bright.
And faltering with strong quiver to its fell.
Drops, slowly rushing, the great outer wall.
From lip to lip a wondering murmur goes.
As crouching a dark moment o'er its prey.
Swiftly again upleaps
The wild flame, and exulting madly glows;
The city burns in an enchanted day.
Still the great throng impassioned silence keeps,
Like an adoring host in ecstasy.
Did ever vision of the opened sky
Entrance more deeply, or did ever voice
Of a just wrath more terribly rejoice?
The houseless beggar gazing has forgot
His hunger; happy lovers' hands relax;
They look no more into each others' eyes.
Wrapt in its mother's shawl
The fretting child no longer cries.
And that soul-piercing flauine
Melts out like wax
The prosperous schemer's busy schemes:
The reveller like a visionary gleams.
An aged wandering pair lift up their heads
Out of old memories; to each, to all.
Time arid the strong world are no more the same.
But threatened, perishable, trembling, brief.
Even as themselves, an instant might destroy.
With all the builded weight of years and grief,
All that old hope and pleasant usage dear.
Glories and dooms before their eyes appear;
Upon their faces joy,

Within their bosoms fear!

Is it that even now
In all, O radiant Desolation, thou
Far off prefigurest
To each obscurely wounded breast
The dream of what shall be?
And in their hearts they see
Rushing in ardent ruin out of sight
With all her splendour, with her streaming robe
Of seas, and her pale peoples, the vast globe
A sullen ember crumble into night!

POEM XXV

TO A DERELICT

O travelled far beyond unhappiness
Into a dreadful peace!
Why tarriest thou here? The street is bright
With noon; the music of the tidal sound
Of London fills the trembling air with power
Flowing and freed around;
No corner but is stirred
With motion and with voices mingling heard.
That every hour
Bring thousand faces trooping into light
Past thee. O hide thyself beneath the ground!
Trouble not our sunshine longer, lest we see
Too clearly inscribed on thee
All that we fear to be.

What dost thou with the sun?
Long since thy race was run.
What spectral task employs
Thy hands? The very boys
That mocked thee, mock no more; they pass thee by,
Like a dumb stone that cannot make reply.
Yet, even as a stone
Will from the turbulent sea
Take voice and motion not its own,
Words on thy lips mechanically stray
With echoes and with gleams that fade and come
Unrecognized, unknown.
And as from some extinguished star
The orphan ray

Still vainly travels its eternal way,
A light of meaning flickers from afar
From what long since was dumb.
Still at the accustomed place
Appears thy ruined face;
And in thy niche all the resounding day,
'Mid busy voices haunting motionless
Thou standest; and to every loitering eye
Resign'st thy history.
Alas! thou also, thou that art so cold,
Thou also once wert young;
And once didst hang upon thy mother's breast
And laugh upon thy father's knee.
But now thy flesh is nearer to the mould
Than the light grass, — and still thou lingerest!
Woe to thee now, because thou chosest ill.
Because each hour thou didst resign
A little more of thy slow-ebbing will.
And to the invading silence didst assent;
Because to Life saying for ever Nay,
To Death thou saidest Yea,
Who leaves thee now engraven with defeat
In this triumphal street.
With all that was and is no longer thine
Yielded and spent
At what a priceless cost,
O face of many battles, and all lost!

Now all thy dues paid. Death possesses thee;
But too secure
To occupy his easy kingdom, spares
To enforce his title; cruelly forbears,
And suffers thee to languish in thy lot,
In this most woeful, that thou weepest not.
So in some street
Stirred with the rushing feet
Of life that glitters and that thunders past.
An aged house, broken and doomed at last.
Ere yet it vanish quite.
Abandons helpless to the light
Spoiled sanctuaries, filled with emptiness.
Where late the weary harboured, and young fears
Were cradled into peace,
And sacred kisses kissed, and private tears
Were dried, and true hearts hid their close delight.
But now the fires are ashes, all is bare.
The torn, gay paper flutters old.
And a phantasmal stair

Climbs into floorless chambers, and hearths cold.

POEM XXVI

TRAFALGAR SQUARE

Slowly the dawn a magic paleness drew
From windows dim; the Pillar high in air
Over dark statues and dumb fountains, threw
A shadow on the solitary square.

They that all night, dozing disquieted,
Huddled together on the benches cold,
Now shrank apart, distrustful and unfed.
And by the growing radiance unconsoled.

Then one, a woman, silently arose.
And came to the broad fountain, brimming cool,
And over the stone margin leaning close.
Dipped hands and bathed her forehead in the pool.

Now as the fresh drops ran upon her brow
And her hands knotted up her hair, the ways
Of old lost mornings came to her, and how
Into her mirror she would smile and gaze.

Then she was troubled; and looked down once more
Into the glimmering water; and she seemed
The very depth of darkness to explore,
If it might yield all that she feared and dreamed.

But that kind clouding mirror answered her
With a soft answer; liquid mysteries
Of shadow, with a pale breeze just astir,
Yielded only the brightness of her eyes.

It was herself; but O what magic wrought
A presage round her, tender and obscure!
The water without stain refused her not:
In that deep vision she rejoined the pure.

The dawn stole on; and from its buried place
Rose in her bosom the sweet strength of youth;
She, the rejected, had no more disgrace:
Her opening heart drew in a different truth.

She that had come past her last hope, and found
Nothing beyond, and had shed no more tears,
But closing with dull ashes her first wound,
Had trodden into the daily dust all fears:

She now began to wonder and to thrill
Upon a new horizon: and the pain
Of hope began to quicken and to fill
The world with strangeness and desire again.

O then I am not come quite to the end,
She murmured, and life holds more than I knew.
Somewhere by seeking I may find a friend
Perhaps, and something in this world be true.

Alone in this bright battle, whose fierce din
Even now awakes round her defenceless lot.
Without home, friend, comfort or peace within.
The very stones might weep her. She weeps not:

But as a plant, that under parching drouth
Thirsted and drooped and daily heavier grew,
Rises afresh to the soft showering south.
She lifts her forehead to the sun anew.

And in her spirit a still fountain springs
Deeper than hunger, faith crying for life,
That to her eyes an inward clearness brings.
And to her heart courage for any strife.

POEM XXVII

THE REFORMER

HYDE PARK

August from a vault of hollow brass
Steep upon the sullen city glares.
Yellower burns the sick and parching grass,
Shivering in the breath of furnace airs.

Prone upon their pale, outwearied brows
Miserable forms lie heavily.
Cumbering the earth; untimely boughs
Fallen from this world-o'ershadowing tree,

London, that with every buried sun
Shakes from her strong life a thousand lives,
Feeds her heart with blood of hearts undone;
Nourished with a million sorrows, thrives.

Hither the Reformer comes; a flame
Burns within his dark, enthusiast gaze.
Still he thirsts to show mankind their shame.
Lift and drag them from their sinful ways.

Now amid the prostrate scattered throng
Standing, he uplifts his earnest cry:
"Wake, awake, rise up from lust and wrong.
Quickly seek God's mercy ere you die!

"Thunder on your hesitation hangs.
God prepares your fearful punishment.
Flee, while yet 'tis time, those endless pangs.
Hearken, wretched sinners, and repent."

Scarce the motion of a listless arm,
Scarce the uneasy lifting of a head,
Answers that stern trumpet of alarm. —
Still he sounds his vehement note of dread.

Hand in hand three children solemn-eyed
Wonder up into his face, and pass.
Often turning backward, o'er the wide
Hueless desert of the hazy grass.

Fierce the lava-torrent of his speech
Pours on those dejected souls around;
Yet his words no single bosom reach.
Wither and fall idle on the ground.

Now at last he falters; his own thought,
His own voice, is strange and far to him.
The sun stares his meaning into naught;
In the stillness all his fire is dim.

From those miserable forms unstirred
Now a mute imploring cry he hears,
Like a stricken creature's, without word;
O what vain voice sounds upon our ears!

Powerless are thy terrors to appal.
Welcome even, so we feel the less
Heavy on our hearts and over all

This intolerable emptiness!

Empty is the earth for us, the skies
Empty; only lives the brazen sun.
Empty are our hearts; and if we rise.
There is nothing to be sought nor won.

If upon our silence thou intrude,
Speak a speech that we may understand!
Leave us to endure our solitude.
Or reach out to us a brother's hand.

Join us to this life that round us teems;
Let us breathe again that common breath!
Bring us sorrow, labour, terrors, dreams,
Madness; but deliver us from death!

POEM XXVIII

WHITECHAPEL HIGH ROAD

Lusty life her river pours
Along a road of shining shores.
The moon of August beams
Mild as upon her harvest slopes; but here
From man's full-breath'd abounding earth
Exiled she walks, as one of alien birth.
The pale, neglected foster-mother of dreams.
For windows with resplendent stores
Along the pavement dazzle and outstare
The booths that front them; there,
To the throng which loiters by in laughing streams
Babble the criers: and 'mid eager sounds
The flaming torches toss to the wind their hair,
And ruddy in trembling waves the light
Flushes cheeks of wondering boys
Assembled, their lips parted and eyes bright,
As the medicine-seller his magic herb expounds,
Or some old man displays his painted toys.
Deaf with a vacant stillness of the tomb,
At intervals a road deserted gapes.
Where night shrinks back into her proper gloom,
Frighted by boisterous flare
Of the flame, that now through a cluster of green grapes
Shines wanly, or on striped apple and smooth pear
Flits blushing; now on rug or carpet spread

In view of the merry buyers, the rude dyes
Re-crimsons, or an antic shadow throws
Over the chestnut brazier's glowing eyes;
And now the sleeping head
Of a gipsy child in his dim corner shows,
Huddled against a canvas wall, his bed
An ancient sack: nor torch, nor hundred cries
Awake him from his sweet profound repose.

But thou, divine moon, with thine equal beam
Dispensing patience, stealest unawares
The thoughts of many that pass sorrowful on
Else undiverted, amid the crowd alone:
Embroiderest with beauties the worn theme
Of trouble; to a fancied harbour calm
Steerest the widow's ship of heavy cares;
And on light spirits of lovers, radiant grown,
Droppest an unimaginable balm.
Yet me to-night thy peace rejoices less
Than this warm human scene, that of rude earth
Pleasantly savours, nor dissembles mirth.
Nor grief nor passion: sweet to me this press
Of life unnumbered, where if hard distress
Be tyrant, hunger is not fed
Nor misery pensioned with the ill-tasting bread
Of pity; but such help as earth ordains
Betwixt her creatures, bound in common pains.
One from another, without prayer, obtains.

POEM XXIX

IN THE BRITISH MUSEUM

Shafts of light, that poured from the August sun,
Glowed on long red walls of the gallery cool;
Fell upon monstrous visions of ages gone,
Still, smiling Sphinx, winged and bearded Bull.

With burnished breast of ebon marble, queen
And king regarded full, from a tranquil brain
Enthroned together, conquered Time; serene
In spite of wisdom, and older than ancient pain.

Hither a poor woman, with sad eyes, came.
And vacantly looked around. The faces vast.
Their strange motionless features, touched with flame,

Awed her: in humble wonder she hurried past;

And shyly beneath a sombre monument sought
Obscurity; into the darkest shade she crept
And rested: soon, diverted awhile, her thought
Returned to its own trouble. At last she slept

Not long sweet sleep alone her spirit possest.
A dream seized her: a solemn and strange dream.
For far from home in an unknown land, opprest
By burning sun, in the noon's terrible beam

She wandered; around her out of the plain arose
Immense Forms, that high above her stared^
Calm they seemed, and used to human woes;
Silent they heard her sorrow, with ears prepared.

Now like a bird, flitting with anxious wings,
Imprisoned within some vast cathedral's aisles.
Hither and thither she flutters: to each she brings
Her prayer, and is answered only with grave smiles.

Indescribably troubled, "Crush me," she cries,
"Speak, speak, or crush me!" The lips are dumb.
— She woke, no longer in shadow, the sun on her eyes,
And sighed, and arose, and returned to her empty home.

POEM XXX

THE THRESHOLD

AN ODE

I walked beside full-flooding Thames to-night
Westward; upon my face the sunset fell:
The hour, the spacious evening, pleased me well.
Buoyant the air breathed after rain, and kind
To senses flattered with soft sound and light
Of merry waves that leapt against the wind.
Where, broadly heaving barge and boat at rest.
The River came at flood; from golden skies
Issuing through arches, black upon the West,
To flame before the sunset's mysteries.

Far off to-night as a remembered dream
That different Thames, familiar as a friend.

That youthful Thames, to whom his willows bend
With private whisper; where my boat would come.
Heaped with fresh flowers, and down the cool smooth stream
Follow his green banks through the twilight home.
Far from these paven shores, these haughty towers.
Where wave and beam glorying together run,
As though they would disown those cradling bowers.
And gushed immediate from the molten sun.

Dazzled I turn; and lo, the solemn East
Before me comes. Soft to my eyes, yet bright,
London her vastness stretches in hushed light
Murmuring; wharf and terrace curve afar
Past bridge and steeple, thronging, great with least.
To Paul's high cross that sparkles like a star.
The distant windows glitter; and high o'er them,
Clouds unapproachable, illumined snows,
Tinged with calm fire that blushes like a gem.
As though themselves burned inwardly, repose.

All things, methought, that inward glory shared,
A radiant strangeness: nothing I beheld
But spoke in a new tongue to me, or spelled
New meanings; and within me a deep sense
Of portals opening, of an hour prepared.
Prophesied; and a light, transported thence,
Of expectation on me also came.
Glowing, the city waits what shall arrive:
The steep clouds smoulder as to sudden flame
They would burst forth, and the wave leaps alive.

Immediately stole over me the thought
Of this age ending; painful and oppressed.
Its cry, entreating still-rejected rest,
Echoed behind me. But I seemed to stand
Beyond; and over the near threshold brought
Of days to be, the air blew strong and bland.
I listened; and a voice, wherein bore part
Cloud, light, and wind, and water, thus began
Atrial tones; a voice from the deep heart
Of all things speaking to the heart of man.

Say, troubled one, what sorrow is it keeps
Thy spirit? Because thy latest dream is shed.
Is the root sapped, and the strong branches dead?
Forget'st thou that thy generations have
Their seasons, and for them her due term sleeps
Spring, with her buds, dreaming in Autumn's grave?

Because 'twas Autumn with thee, thou sit'st mute.
To the fall of the leaf consenting: Yet thine eyes
Cast round thee, and consider what fair fruit
The full seeds bear in charge! Wake, and arise!

Wake, and for blither energy remit
This tedious questing in the inscrutable past,
This pondering the before and after vast.
O couldst thou take, like us. Time's quiet bloom,
On life alone expend thy freshened wit.
The burden and the joy alone resume!
The mountains groan not that the streams devour
With thievish tongue their ancient high estate,
Nor of her pining leaf complains the flower;
But thou enjoy'st not nor reject'st thy fate.

Pitying thee, the Powers that on thee cast
Thy destiny, 'mid labour solace sent.
For veiled they keep that infinite ascent
Of years, and by degrees the pathway show
Up which thou mountest, deeming still the last
Step won, and numbered all the stones of woe.
And easily triumphant thou lean'st forth
To grasp the final palm; when that eludes,
As easily dejected: placid Earth
Remains, a mirror for thy hundred moods.

Dream-builder, for whose dreams thy lips invent
Names of sweet sound, freedom and peace and truth.
Upon the bright fermenting mists of youth
Projecting a foredoomed reality:
Happy, if gross joys could thy brain content.
Or could thy faith match thy credulity;
Ever inweaving Earth's plain warp with thread
Of thy deep wishes, thine own heart's strong hue.
The mind thy prison, thought thy narrow bed.
With truth, with freedom what hast thou to do?

O yet, I answered, not in vain desire
Spurs us to gaze into the infinity.
To dip our hands in that wide whispering sea.
How shall one flower the whole wood's voices tell,
Or one small sphere interpret that full choir
Of orb with orb, music ineffable
From all worlds mingled? Yet since our best joy
Not in possession but beyond us lies.
Our hearts at last, weary of earth's annoy,
Only that far-off music satisfies.

Name beyond names. Heart of the Eternal Life,
Whom our faint thought hardly at times conceives,
Who hear'st but as the oak his fluttered leaves
The cry of parting spirits; who in the pang
For children born rejoicest; from whose strife
And travail issuing the bright worlds outsprang;
If the wide thought of thee my childish grief
Ever effaced, accept my manhood's vow!
O sweet and insupportable, O chief
And first and last of all loves, hear me now!

Me, whom this living vastness once appalled.
And this uproar disheartened and oppressed.
Now larger thoughts enfranchise, with sweet zest
Nourish, and this immensity sustains;
Buoyed as a swimmer upon ocean, called
From time to the eternal, my due pains
Accepting, in thy bosom I repose.
Of joys and griefs together make my bed,
In longing to set sure against all foes
My spirit freed, and with thy spirit wed.

Thou, thou remainest ever in lovely power
Triumphant, whom beginning never knew;
'Tis we alone that our own strength undo,
'Tis we alone that, to thy ardour lame,
Often defeated, miserably deflower
The joy thou gavest, quench the imparted flame.
And native sweet sourly to ashes turn.
O help, inspire! Us with thyself endow!
Through our brief actions let thy greatness burn.
As through the clouds the light is burning now!

For me, since thou this hour to see thee whole
Vouchsafest, no more shall my heart deny
That thou proceed'st, because I fail and cry.
Henceforth will I endure to walk right on
Nor my bliss too much ponder, nor my dole.
And since dear peace fortifies faith alone,
I trust thee, and not loth resign my heart,
Nor though thou shouldst betray me, wound and rend,
Would my course alter, that the better part
Have chosen, enduring to the unknown end.

So inwardly my lifted spirit sang.
And lo, that solemn joy to authorize.
With answering bloom before my lifted eyes

The clouds moved softly; the far western fires
A moment o'er the steeples paused and sprang.
Now on the eye the fading light expires.
But 'tis to me as if Earth cast off Day,
Assuming her own glory, and her flight
Unwearied urging on the eternal way.
Already glowed among the lamps of Night.

POEM XXXI

THE ROAD MENDERS

How solitary gleams the lamplit street
Waiting the far-off morn!
How softly from the unresting city blows
The murmur borne
Down this deserted way!
Dim loiterers pass home with stealthy feet.
Now only, sudden at their interval,
The lofty chimes awaken and let fall
Deep thrills of ordered sound;
Subsiding echoes gradually drowned
In a great stillness, that creeps up around,
And darkly grows
Profounder over all
Like a strong frost, hushing a stormy day.

But who is this, that by the brazier red
Encamped in his rude hut.
With many a sack about his shoulder spread
Watches with eyes unshut?
The burning brazier flushes his old face,
Illumining the old thoughts in his eyes.
Surely the Night doth to her secrecies
Admit him, and the watching stars attune
To their high patience, who so lightly seems
To bear the weight of many thousand dreams
(Dark hosts around him sleeping numberless);
He surely hath unbuilt all walls of thought
To reach an air-wide wisdom, past access
Of us, who labour in the noisy noon.
The noon that knows him not.

For lo, at last the gloom slowly retreats.
And swiftly, like an army, comes the Day,
All bright and loud through the awakened streets

Sending a cheerful hum,
And he has stolen away.
Now, with the morning shining round them, come
Young men, and strip their coats
And loose the shirts about their throats,
And lightly up their ponderous hammers lift,
Each in his turn descending swift
With triple strokes that answer and begin
Duly, and quiver in repeated change.
Marrying the eager echoes that weave in
A music clear and strange.
But pausing soon, each lays his hammer down
And deeply breathing bares
His chest, stalwart and brown.
To the sunny airs.
Laughing one to another, limber hand
On limber hip, flushed in a group they stand.
And now untired renew their ringing toil.

The sun stands high, and ever a fresh throng
Comes murmuring; but that eddying turmoil
Leaves many a loiterer, prosperous or unfed.
On easy or unhappy ways
At idle gaze.
Charmed in the sunshine and the rhythm enthralling,
As of unwearied Fates, for ever young.
That on the anvil of necessity
From measureless desire and quivering fear.
With musical sure lifting and downfalling
Of arm and hammer driven perpetually,
Beat out in obscure span
The fiery destiny of man.

POEM XXXII

NOVEMBER

Together we laughed and talked in the warm lit room:
Out now, alone I come
Into the street, in the fell of the early night.
Shadowy skies, with a pale uncertain gloom,
Hover above the houses dim; but bright
In wetness mirrored far.
Retreating lamps outshine the lingering light.
Hazily blue the air, heavy with dews
The wind; and before me the cries and the crowd.

And the sleepless murmur of wheels; not loud,
For a magical softness all imbrues.
The softness estranges my sense: I see and I hear,
But know 'tis a vision intangible, shapes that seem.
All is unreal; the sound of the felling of feet,
Coming figures, and far-off hum of the street;
A dream, the gliding hurry, the endless lights.
Houses and sky, a dream, a dream!

POEM XXXIII

THE MOTHER

The Mother to her brooding breast
Her shrouded baby closely holds,
A stationary shadow, drest
In shadow, felling folds on folds.

With gesture motionless as Night
She stands; through wavering glare and sound
Deep pierces like a sombre light
The full gloom of her gaze profound.

POEM XXXIV

THE TOY SELLER

The Toy-seller his idle wares
Carefully ranges, side by side;
With coveting soft earnest airs
The children linger, open-eyed.

His haunted soul from far away
Looks in the lamplight absently:
They see not him, O happy they!
He sees not them, O woeful he!

POEM XXXV

THE BIRCH TREE

Touched with beauty, I stand still and gaze

In the autumn twilight. Yellow leaves and brown,
The grass enriching, gleam, or waver down
From lime and elm: far-glimmering through the haze
The quiet lamps in order twinkle; dumb
And fair the park lies; faint the city's hum.

And I regret not June's impassioned prime.
When her deep lilies banqueted the air.
And this now ruined, then so fragrant lime
Cooled with clear green the heavy noon's high glare;
Nor flushed carnations, breathing hot July;
Nor April's thrush in the blithest songs of the year.
With brown bloom on the elms and dazzling sky;
So strange a charm there lingers in this austere
Resigning month, yielding to what must be.
Yet most, O delicate birch, I envy thee.
Child among trees! with silvery slender limbs
And purple sprays of drooping hair. Night dims
The grass; the great elms darken; no birds sing.
At last I sigh for the warmth and the fragrance flown.
But thou in the leafless twilight shinest alone.
Awaiting in ignorant trust the certain spring.

POEM XXXVI

FOG

Magically awakened to a strange, brown night
The streets lie cold. A hush of heavy gloom
Dulls the noise of the wheels to a murmur dead:
Near and sudden the passing figures loom;
And out of darkness steep on startled sight
The topless walls in apparition emerge.
Nothing revealing but their own thin flames,
The rayless lamps burn faint and bleared and red:
Link-boys' cries, and the shuffle of horses led,
Pierce the thick air; and like a distant dirge.
Melancholy horns wail from the shrouded Thames.
Long the blind morning hooded the dumb town;
Till lo! in an instant winds arose, and the air
Lifted: at once, from a cold and spectral sky
Appears the sun, and laughs in mockery down
On groping travellers far from where they deem,
In unconjectured roads; the dwindled stream
Of traffic in slow confusion crawling by:
The baffled hive of helpless man laid bare.

MOTHER OF EXILES

What far-off trouble steals
In soft-blown drifts of glimmering rain?
What is it the wind feels,
What sighing of what old home-seeking pain
Among the hurried footsteps and the wheels,
The living low continual roar
Of night and London? What is it comes near.
Felt like a blind man's touch along the wall
Questing, and strange, like fear.
Lets a lone silence 'mid the turmoil fall.
Makes the long street seem vaster than before.
And the tall lamp, above dim passers-by,
Gleam solitary as on an ocean shore.

Ships on for tracks are stemming through the night;
South, east and west by foreign stars they steer;
Another half-world in the sun lies bright;
The darkness and the wind are here.

And now the rare late footfall scarce is heard.
But the wind cries along the emptied street.
In cowering lamp-light flicker the fine drops
To vanish wildly blurred;
A hunted sky flies over the housetops.
Importunate gusts beat
Shaking the windows, knocking at the doors
As with phantasmal hands,
A crying as of spirits from far shores
And the bright under-lands,
Seeking one place
That is to each eternal in the hue
The light, the shadow of some certain hour,
One pang-like moment, years cannot efface.
O infinite remoteness, near and new!
O corner where friend parted from his friend!
O door of the first kiss, the last embrace!
O day when all was possible, O end
Irrevocable! O dream-feet that pace
One street, dear to the dead!
O London stones, that glimmer in the rain,
With bliss, with pain, have you not also bled?

JOHN WINTER

What ails John Winter, that so oft
Silent he sits apart?
The neighbours cast their looks on him;
But deep he hides his heart.

In Deptford streets the houses small
Huddle forlorn together.
Whether the wind blow or be still,
'Tis soiled and sorry weather.

But over these dim roofs arise
Tall masts of ocean ships,
Whenever John Winter looked on them
The salt blew on his lips.

He cannot pace the street about,
But they stand before his eyes!
The more he shuns them, the more proud
And beautiful they rise.

He turns his head, but in his ear
The steady Trade-winds run,
And in his eye the endless waves
Ride on into the sun.

His little boy at evening said,
Now tell us, Dad, a tale
Of naked men that shoot with bows,
Tell of the spouting whale!

He told old tales, his eyes were bright,
His wife looked up to see
And smiled on him: but in the midst
He ended suddenly.

He bade them each good-night, and kissed
And held them to his breast.
They wondered and were still, to feel
Their lips so fondly pressed.

He sat absorbed in silent gloom.

His wife lifted her head
From sewing, and stole up to him.
What ails you, John? she said.

He spoke no word. A silent tear
Fell softly down her cheek.
She knelt beside him, and his hand
Was on her forehead meek.

But even as his tender touch
Her dumb distress consoled.
The mighty waves danced in his eyes
And through the silence rolled.

There fell a soft November night,
Restless with gusts that shook
The chimneys, and beat wildly down
The flames in the chimney nook.

John Winter lay beside his wife.
'Twas past the mid of night.
Softly he rose, and in dead hush
Stood stealthily upright.

Softly he came where slept his boys,
And kissed them in their bed.
One stretched his arms out in his sleep:
At that he turned his head.

And now he bent above his wife.
She slept a sleep serene.
Her patient soul was in the peace
Of breathing slumber seen.

At last he kissed one aching kiss,
Then shrank again in dread,
And from his own home guiltily
And like a thief he fled.

But now with darkness and the wind
He breathes a breath more free,
And walks with calmer step like one
Who goes with destiny.

And see, before him the great masts
Tower with all their spars
Black on the dimness, soaring bold
Among the mazy stars.

In stormy rushings through the air
Wild scents the darkness filled,
And with a fierce forgetfulness
His drinking nostril thrilled.

He hasted with quick feet, he hugged
The wildness to his breast,
As one who goes the only way
To set his heart at rest.

When morning glimmered, a great ship
Dropt gliding down the shore.
John Winter coiled the anchor ropes
Among his mates once more.

POEM XXXIX

SONGS OF THE WORLD UNBORN

Songs of the world unborn
Swelling within me, a shoot from the heart of Spring,
As I walk the ample and teeming street
This tranquil and misty morn,
What is it to me you sing?

My body warm, my brain clear.
Unreasoning joy possesses my soul complete;
The keen air mettles my blood,
And the pavement rings to my feet,

O houses erect and vast, O steeples proud.
That soar serenely aloof.
Vistas of railing and roof.
Dim-seen in the delicate shroud of the frosty air,
You are built but of shadow and cloud,
I will come with the wind and blow,
You shall melt, to be seen no longer, O phantoms fair.
Embattled city, trampler of dreams,
So long deluding, thou shalt delude no more;
The trembling heart thou haughtily spurnest,
But thou from a dream art sprung,
From a far-off vision of yore,
To a dream, to a dream returnest.
Time, the tarrier,
Time the unshunnable.

Stealing with patient rivers the mountainous lands.
Or in turbulent fire upheaving,
Who shifts for ever the sands,
Who gently breaks the unbreakable barrier,
Year upon year into broadening silence weaving,
Time, O mighty and mightily peopled city.
Time is busy with thee.
Behold, the tall tower moulders in air.
The staunch beam crumbles to earth,
Pinnacles falter and fall.
And the immemorial wall
Melts, as a cloud is melted under the sun.
Nor these alone, but alas,
Things of diviner birth,
Glories of men and women strong and fair.
They too, alas, perpetually undone!
As the green apparition of leaves
Buds out in the smile of May;
As the red leaf smoulders away.
That frozen Earth receives;
In all thy happy, in all thy desolate places.
They spring, they glide.
Unnumbered blooming and fading faces!
O what shall abide?
Aching desire, mutinous longing,
Love, the divine rebel, the challenge of all.
Faith, that the doubters doubted and wept her fall,
To an empty sepulchre thronging:
These, the sap of the earth,
Irresistibly sprung,
In the blood of heroes running sweet.
In the dream of the dreamers ever young.
Supplanting the solid and vast delusions,
Hearten the heart of the wronged to endure defeat,
The forward-gazing eyes of the old sustain.
Mighty in perishing youth, and in endless birth.
These remain.

Robert Laurence Binyon, CH, was born on August 10th, 1869 in Lancaster in Lancashire, England to Quaker parents, Frederick Binyon and Mary Dockray.

He studied at St Paul's School, London before enrolling at Trinity College, Oxford, to read classics.

Binyon's first published work was Persephone in 1890. Whilst only a few pages in length it certainly illustrated the talents that Binyon would develop as a poet even though he continued to advance multiple career opportunities.

Immediately after graduating in 1893, Binyon started work at the British Museum for the Department of Printed Books, writing catalogues for the museum and art monographs for himself. As well as being one of England's best poets he was also renowned for his knowledge of various arts particularly with regard to Japan and Persia.

His first poetry book Lyric Poems was published in 1894.

In 1895 his first art book, Dutch Etchers of the Seventeenth Century, was published and, that same year, Binyon moved into the Museum's Department of Prints and Drawings.

Whilst Binyon became known to a wide audience as a poet his output was not prodigious. In 1898, Porphyrion & Other Poems was published followed by Odes (1901) and The Death of Adam & Other Poems (1904).

That same year, 1904, Binyon married the historian Cicely Margaret Powell. The union was to produce three daughters.

In the early years of the 20th Century Binyon was a regular patron of the Wiener Cafe of London together with fellow artists and intellectuals; Ezra Pound, Sir William Rothenstein, Walter Sickert, Charles Ricketts, Lucien Pissarro and Edmund Dulac.

His poetic work continued despite the demands of the British Museum and his other interests. London Visions was published in 1908 followed by England & Other Poems in 1909.

His work at the British Museum ensured promotions were a frequent occurrence for Binyon. In 1909, he became its Assistant Keeper, and in 1913 he was made the Keeper of the new Sub-Department of Oriental Prints and Drawings.

It was also at this time that he played a crucial role in the formation of Modernism in London by introducing young Imagist poets such as Ezra Pound, Richard Aldington and H.D. (Hilda Doolittle) to East Asian visual art and literature.

Many of Binyon's books produced while at the Museum were influenced by his own sensibilities as a poet, although some are clearly works of plain scholarship, such as his four volume catalogue of all the Museum's English drawings, and his seminal catalogue of Chinese and Japanese prints.

Binyon's poetic reputation before the war, although built on several slim volumes, was such that, on the death of the Poet Laureate Alfred Austin in 1913, Binyon was among the names considered as his likely successor. It was quite a field. Among the other illustrious contenders were Thomas Hardy, John Masefield and Rudyard Kipling; however the post was awarded to Robert Bridges.

Moved and shaken by the onset of the World War I and its military tactics of young men slaughtered to hold or gain a few yards of shell-shocked mud as the British Expeditionary Force began its campaign Binyon wrote his seminal poem For the Fallen, with its Ode of Remembrance (the third and fourth or simply the fourth stanza of the poem). The poem was published by The Times newspaper on September 21st, when public feeling was shaken by the recent Battle of Marne. It became an instant classic, turning moments of great loss into a National and human tribute.

Today, For the Fallen, is often recited at Remembrance Sunday services as well as being an integral part of Anzac Day services in Australia and New Zealand and of November 11th Remembrance Day services in Canada. The "Ode of Remembrance" is now acknowledged as a tribute to all casualties of war, irrespective of nation.

In 1915, despite being too old to enlist, Binyon volunteered at a British hospital for French soldiers, the Hôpital Temporaire d'Arc-en-Barrois, Haute-Marne, France, working for a short time as a hospital orderly.

He returned there in the summer of 1916 and took care of soldiers taken in from the Verdun battlefield. He wrote about his experiences in For Dauntless France (1918) and his poems, "Fetching the Wounded" and "The Distant Guns", were inspired by his hospital service.

After the war, he returned to the British Museum and wrote numerous books on art; especially on William Blake, Persian and Japanese art. His work on ancient Japanese and Chinese cultures offered inspiration that inspired many, among them the poets Ezra Pound and W. B. Yeats. His work on Blake and his followers kept alive the then nearly-forgotten memory of the work of Samuel Palmer. Binyon's spectrum of interests continued the traditional interest of British visionary Romanticism in the rich strangeness of Mediterranean and Oriental cultures.

In 1931, his two volume Collected Poems appeared and by 1932, Binyon was promoted to the post of Keeper of the Prints and Drawings Department. The following year, 1933, he retired from the British Museum. He went to live in the country at Westridge Green, near Streatley but continued writing poetry.

In 1933–1934, Binyon was appointed Norton Professor of Poetry at Harvard University. He delivered a series of lectures on The Spirit of Man in Asian Art, which were published in 1935.

Binyon continued his academic work: in May, 1939 he gave the prestigious Romanes Lecture in Oxford on Art and Freedom, and in 1940 he was appointed the Byron Professor of English Literature at the University of Athens. He worked there until forced to leave by the German invasion of Greece in April, 1941.

Binyon had been friends with Ezra Pound for a long time, and in the 1930s the two became especially close; Pound affectionately called him "BinBin", and he assisted Binyon with his translation of Dante.

Between 1933 and 1943, Binyon published his acclaimed translation of Dante's Divine Comedy in an English version of terza rima, made with some editorial assistance by Ezra Pound. It was acknowledged for many decades as *the* popular translation for Dante readers.

During the horrors of the Second World War Binyon wrote a poem that many claim as to be a masterpiece 'The Burning of the Leaves', puts in print his lines on the London Blitz.

At his death Binyon was working on a major three-part Arthurian trilogy, the first part of which was published after his death as The Madness of Merlin (1947).

Robert Laurence Binyon died in Dunedin Nursing Home, Bath Road, Reading, on March 10th, 1943 after undergoing an operation. A funeral service was held at Trinity College Chapel, Oxford, on March 13th, 1943.

Binyon's ashes were scattered at St. Mary's Church, Aldworth.

On November 11th, 1985, Binyon was among sixteen poets of the Great War commemorated on a slate stone unveiled in Westminster Abbey's Poets' Corner. The inscription on the stone quotes a fellow Great War poet, Wilfred Owen. It reads: "My subject is War, and the pity of War. The Poetry is in the pity."

Laurence Binyon – A Concise Bibliography

Poems and Verse
Persephone (1890)
Lyric Poems (1894)
The Praise of Life (1896)
Porphyrion & Other Poems (1898)
Odes (1901)
Death of Adam & Other Poems (1904)
Penthesilea (1905)
London Visions (1908)
England & Other Poems (1909)
Auguries (1913)
For The Fallen (The Times, September 21st, 1914)
The Winnowing Fan (1914)
The Anvil (1916)
The Cause (1917)
The New World: Poems (1918)
The Secret: Sixty Poems (1920)
The Idols (1928)
Collected Poems Vol I: London Visions, Narrative Poems, Translations (1931)
Collected Poems Vol II: Lyrical Poems (1931)
The North Star & Other Poems (1941)
The Burning of the Leaves & Other Poems (1944)
The Madness of Merlin (1947)

Poems Set to Music
In 1915 Cyril Rootham set "For the Fallen" for chorus and orchestra, first performed in 1919 by the Cambridge University Musical Society conducted by the composer.

Edward Elgar set to music "The Fourth of August", "To Women", and "For the Fallen", as The Spirit of England, Op. 80, for tenor or soprano solo, chorus and orchestra (1917).

English Arts and Myth
Dutch Etchers of the Seventeenth Century (1895), Binyon's first book on painting
John Crone and John Sell Cotman (1897)
William Blake: Being all his Woodcuts Photographically Reproduced in Facsimile (1902)
English Poetry in its relation to painting and the other arts (1918)
Drawings and Engravings of William Blake (1922)
Arthur: A Tragedy (1923)
The Followers of William Blake (1925)
The Engraved Designs of William Blake (1926)
Landscape in English Art and Poetry (1931)
English Watercolours (1933)
Gerard Hopkins and his influence (1939)
Art and freedom. (The Romanes lecture, delivered 25 May 1939). Oxford: The Clarendon press, (1939)

Japanese and Persian Arts
Painting in the Far East (1908)
Japanese Art (1909)
Flight of the Dragon (1911)
The Court Painters of the Grand Moguls (1921)
Japanese Colour Prints (1923)
The Poems of Nizami (1928) (Translation)
Persian Miniature Painting (1933)
The Spirit of Man in Asian Art (1936)
Autobiography[edit]
For Dauntless France (1918) (War memoir)

Biography
Botticelli (1913)
Akbar (1932)

Stage Plays
Brief Candles A verse-drama about the decision of Richard III to dispatch his two nephews
Paris and Œnone. A Tragedy in One Act (1906)
Godstow Nunnery: Play
Boadicea; A Play in eight Scenes
Attila: A Tragedy in Four Acts (1907)
Ayuli: A Play in three Acts and an Epilogue
Sophro the Wise: A Play for Children
(Most of the above were written for John Masefield's theatre).